T0318315

Rational Emotive Behaviour Therapy

This straightforward guide introduces the newcomer to the core theoretical principles and therapeutic strategies of Rational Emotive Behaviour Therapy (REBT). Starting with the ABC model of emotion popularized by Albert Ellis from the outset when he developed his approach to CBT, the guide then shows how REBT distinguishes between unhealthy and healthy negative emotions. From there it outlines the four irrational attitudes theorized to be at the core of emotional and behavioural disturbance. Finally, the newcomer to REBT will develop an appreciation for how REBT inoculates clients against future problems and teaches them to maintain and extend their treatment gains.

This *Newcomer's Guide* will be a useful contribution to counsellors and psychotherapists in training, either in Rational Emotive Behaviour Therapy or another cognitive-behavioural approach.

Walter J. Matweychuk, Ph.D., is in full-time clinical practice at the University of Pennsylvania in Philadelphia, USA and trains doctoral students in Rational Emotive Behaviour Therapy. He has worked with Drs. Ellis and Beck and is well informed in the similarities and important differences between these two pioneering forms of Cognitive Behaviour Therapy. He maintains a private practice and is an adjunct professor in applied psychology at New York University where he teaches Cognitive Behaviour Therapy to graduate students. He is co-author, with Windy Dryden, of *Overcoming Your Addictions* and *Rational Emotive Behaviour Therapy: A Newcomer's Guide*. To learn more about Rational Emotive Behaviour Therapy, go to: REBTDoctor.com

Windy Dryden, Ph.D., is in part-time clinical and consultative practice and is an international authority on Cognitive Behaviour Therapy. He is Emeritus Professor of Psychotherapeutic Studies at Goldsmiths, University of London. He has worked in psychotherapy for more than 40 years and is the author and editor of over 215 books.

Routledge Focus on Mental Health

Routledge Focus on Mental Health presents short books on current topics, linking in with cutting-edge research and practice.
For a full list of titles in this series, please visit https://www.routledge.com/Routledge-Focus-on-Mental-Health/book-series/RFMH

Titles in the series:

Working with Interpreters in Psychological Therapy: The Right to be Understood
Jude Boyles and Nathalie Talbot

Rational Emotive Behaviour Therapy: A Newcomer's Guide
Walter J. Matweychuk and Windy Dryden

The Feldenkrais Method for Executive Coaches, Managers, and Business Leaders: Moving in All Directions
Paul Ogden and Garet Newell

Rational Emotive Behaviour Therapy
A Newcomer's Guide

Walter J. Matweychuk and Windy Dryden

Routledge
Taylor & Francis Group

LONDON AND NEW YORK

First published 2017 by Routledge

2 Park Square, Milton Park, Abingdon, Oxfordshire OX14 4RN

52 Vanderbilt Avenue, New York, NY 10017

Routledge is an imprint of the Taylor & Francis Group, an informa business

First issued in paperback 2019

British Library Cataloguing in Publication Data
A catalogue record for this book is available from the British Library

Library of Congress Cataloging in Publication Data
A catalog record for this book has been requested

ISBN: 978-1-138-05703-6 (hbk)
ISBN: 978-0-367-88861-9 (pbk)

Typeset in Times New Roman
by Swales & Willis Ltd, Exeter, Devon, UK

To my wife, Pam, whose love, wit, and very fine meals are constants in my life.

To my wife, Louise, for her love and support and for showing an attitude of discomfort tolerance for my many foibles.

Contents

Introduction

In a 1956 presentation at the American Psychological Association's conference in Chicago, Albert Ellis argued that illogical ideas and philosophies were the basic causes of emotional disturbance. This presentation was subsequently published in 1958 in the Journal of General Psychology. It was titled *Rational Therapy*. Ellis, the field's first cognitive therapist, delineated and examined twelve irrational ideas. Through his clinical work, Ellis came to see that philosophical attitudes were the foundation for self-defeating emotions and behaviours. Adding credibility to his pioneering view, Aaron T. Beck later published *Thinking and Depression* in the Archives of General Psychiatry in 1963. By this point in time, he too had come to see that thinking played a significant role in clinical depression.

Over the past sixty years, the initial theory and therapeutic practice Ellis suggested have been renamed. More importantly, these principles and clinical strategies have been significantly refined. In 1961, Ellis called his approach Rational-Emotive Therapy (RET) to emphasize the emotive aspects of his treatment. In 1993 he rebranded his system of psychotherapy as Rational Emotive Behaviour Therapy (REBT) to highlight his longstanding use of behavioural interventions. Ellis's pioneering and comprehensive form of cognitive behavioural therapy (CBT) continues to be empirically tested and theoretically refined by a global community of clinicians and researchers. Every day these practitioners help clients to help themselves. The client achieves relief from suffering by being shown how they are responsible for their emotions and that they *largely disturb themselves* about adversity by clinging to rigid and extreme attitudes. REBT attracts new practitioners because it is an efficient, evidence-based cognitive-behavioural psychotherapy that is applicable to a wide range of clinical problems plaguing adults, adolescents and children. REBT has been applied to emotional disorders involving depression, anxiety and anger as well as behavioural disorders like substance abuse and a lack of self-discipline. REBT can be applied to psychiatric disorders, as well as a very wide variety of problems of everyday living.

Recently, there has been increasing interest in positive psychology. Consistent with this zeitgeist, REBT not only facilitates the alleviation of emotional disturbance, but also promotes psychological health. More so than any other CBT approach, REBT is explicit about what constitutes emotional health and how to gain it, as well as how to find personal happiness.

This guide introduces the newcomer to the core theoretical principles and therapeutic strategies of REBT. Our experience has shown that once newcomers get an accurate introduction to these core principles and practices they become quite eager to obtain further training in REBT.

We start with the ABC model of emotion that Ellis (1962) popularized from the outset when he developed his approach to CBT. The guide then shows how REBT distinguishes between unhealthy and healthy negative emotions. Novices often do not know what is meant by a rational attitude in REBT. We will clearly define what is meant by the word rational in REBT. From there you will come to understand the four irrational attitudes theorized to be at the core of emotional and behavioural disturbance.

By reading this guide, you will come to understand how the REBT practitioner facilitates both intellectual insight and emotional change. Finally, the newcomer to REBT will develop an appreciation for how REBT inoculates clients against future problems and teaches them to maintain and extend their treatment gains.

We hope that this guide will be the first step you take on your journey to learn REBT. Welcome, newcomer!

1 REBT's distinctive ABC model of emotion

REBT's distinctive model

REBT has a distinctive ABC model. Dryden (2015) has called this the situational ABC model of emotional disturbance. Here, the person is in an actual situation and infers what is going on in the world at A, brings to this inference basic attitudes at point B and experiences consequences at C. These are consequential emotions, behaviours (overt or inclinations to act) and subsequent distorted cognitions similar to Beck's (1976) cognitive distortions. Note that cognitions occur at all three points of REBT's distinctive ABC model. According to this ABC model, in psychological disturbance, the cognitions at A and C tend to be biased inferences while the key cognitions at B are rigid and extreme basic attitudes.

Clients typically enter therapy with an incomplete version of the generic ABC model. They know about their adversity at A and how they respond at C, but they tend to be unaware of the role cognition plays at point B in the ABC model. With this A–C model, clients are at a disadvantage to cope with the adversities they face. The A–C model invites three ways of coping. These are to change the A, avoid the A or to attempt not to feel the C through various escape behaviours and poor choices. All three strategies have disadvantages as a first line of defence.

Note that not all problems at A can be changed quickly or at all. Furthermore, avoiding A may have significant drawbacks. For example, if A is a job-related adversity, consider for a moment the downside of choosing to cope with this adversity by not reporting to work due to one's emotional disturbance at point C. Is this feasible?

Secondly, making the choice not to feel the disturbed emotion at C is often equally problematic. Ingestion of psychoactive substances works temporarily, but after they are metabolized the relief afforded goes away. Behaviours like exercise, sexual activity and eating all can be powerfully distractive, but if used to excess, inappropriately or in an unhealthy way, they can produce their own problems.

Initially addressing basic attitudes

REBT helps clients to liberate themselves by addressing their rigid and extreme basic attitudes at point B about what they infer is going on at point A. Clients are shown that events do not directly cause self-defeating emotions and behaviours at point C. This is an epiphany to many clients.

REBT shows clients that, upon examination, rigid and extreme attitudes are the proximal link to disturbance. Said another way, REBT shows clients that adverse events (at A) do not directly cause emotional disturbance (at C). When these adversities occur, clients have a choice of what basic attitudes to adopt towards A. If they adopt a set of rigid and extreme attitudes (at B) towards the adversity, then they will disturb themselves (at C) emotionally, behaviourally and cognitively. However, if they adopt a set of flexible and non-extreme attitudes (at B) towards the same adversity, they will respond to it in a constructive manner, emotionally, behaviourally and cognitively. Therefore, the REBT model holds that the client is responsible for their basic attitudes at point B and the subsequently produced disturbed feelings, behaviours and downstream cognitive distortions at point C.

Application to events of the past

The REBT model is very useful when clients are disturbed about past events. When people hold inferences at A about past events, REBT's ABC model can be liberating. Events of the past cannot be changed. Clients sometimes believe that emotional disturbance experienced in the present is the result of unchangeable past events. REBT shows clients that a more liberating model is that present basic attitudes at B about past events maintain emotional disturbance about past events. By modifying current attitudes, clients can liberate themselves from the disturbance that has been tied to distant adverse events.

Application to future events

REBT's model also applies to inferences made in the present about anticipated future events. When people make inferences at A about future events, they may hold rigid and extreme basic attitudes at point B, which sets the stage for emotional disturbance in the present. By teaching clients the ABC model of REBT and helping them to adopt it, REBT inoculates clients against future adversities that might occur. Relinquishing currently held rigid and extreme attitudes towards possible future adversity increases the chance of more accurate informational processing as the future comes into the present. Said another way, rational attitudes towards the future increase the chances of perceiving reality more accurately as it unfolds.

It is important to note the great advantages that REBT's model offers. Often, adversities at point A are slow to change, require persistent effort to modify or are so challenging that only poor options are available. When one adopts the REBT model, change at point B will produce emotional improvement at point C even when A is slow to change, cannot be modified or can only be imperfectly addressed. Adoption of the REBT model offers emotional leverage which clients probably didn't utilize before exposure to REBT. Eliminating emotional disturbance about adverse events enables client persistence, creative problem-solving and skilful execution of the selected strategies clients choose to attempt to change A.

Therapists also profit from the adoption of the ABC model in ways similar to clients. Therapists often encounter client resistance which can be viewed as an A. Therapists who adopt the ABC model avoid emotional disturbance at point C, which interferes with the execution of interventions for addressing resistance, by developing and holding a set of flexible and non-extreme attitudes towards client resistance at B. A therapist who has truly adopted an attitudinal system based on flexibility and being non-extreme becomes an authentic role model of the approach, and is more likely to display creativity in addressing client resistance. In so doing, they have a better chance of helping the client.

In the next chapter we will make clear REBT's position on the distinction between unhealthy and healthy negative emotions.

2 Unhealthy and healthy negative emotions

Characteristics of unhealthy and healthy negative emotions

Unhealthy and healthy negative emotions share the characteristic that they are both negative in tone. The distinction between these two groups of emotions is not their tone, but the functionality of behaviour and degree of realism in thinking that co-occur at point C.

Unhealthy negative emotions and self-defeating behaviour

REBT teaches that unhealthy negative emotions stemming from rigid and extreme attitudes are dysfunctional because they co-occur with behaviour that tends to be self-defeating. People experiencing unhealthy negative emotions usually do not solve problems as effectively as they would if they were experiencing healthier negative emotions. Unhealthy negative emotions are more likely to be associated with extreme behaviour (e.g. shouting in the case of unhealthy anger), impulsive or short-sighted behaviour, a lack of persistence or a lack of creative problem solving.

Unhealthy negative emotions and cognitive consequences

The rigid and extreme attitudes that spawn unhealthy negative emotions may also produce negative cognitive consequences. Cognitive distortions like jumping to conclusions, mind reading and overgeneralization, among others, are more likely to co-occur when a client is holding a rigid and/or extreme attitude. These cognitive distortions will tend to interfere with the client's quality of thinking needed to attain important goals in the face of adversity.

If clients are shown how to respond to adversity with healthy negative emotions through holding a set of flexible and non-extreme attitudes, it is likely that these emotions will be associated with constructive behavioural and cognitive responses resulting in increased resiliency and effort to achieve one's goals.

Negative emotions and terminology

Dryden (2015) noted the limited word choices in English for negative emotions and proposed eight different labels for the unhealthy and healthy negative emotions. The labels proposed are shown in Table 2.1.

From a therapeutic perspective, what is important is not that therapist and client use the terminology proposed in Table 2.1, but that they employ terms that discriminate between healthy and unhealthy negative emotions which make sense to the client.

Inferential themes of unhealthy negative emotions

Dryden (2009), drawing on the work of Beck (1976), delineated the typical inferences at A that are associated with each of the eight basic unhealthy negative emotions at C. Newcomers to REBT would be well advised to acquaint themselves with

Table 2.1 Unhealthy negative emotions (UNEs) and healthy negative emotions (HNEs) in RBT theory.

Unhealthy Negative Emotions (UNEs)	Healthy Negative Emotions (UNEs)
Anxiety	Concern
Depression	Sadness
Guilt	Remorse
Shame	Disappointment
Hurt	Sorrow
Unhealthy (dysfunctional) anger	Healthy (functional) anger
Unhealthy (dysfunctional) jealousy	Healthy (functional) jealousy
Unhealthy (dysfunctional) envy	Healthy (functional) envy

these inferential themes, as this will enhance diagnostic skill when assessing both the A and C of a client's emotional episode. In Table 2.2, you will see the eight basic Unhealthy Negative Emotions and their inferential themes at A.

Note that our language does not provide words for labelling both the unhealthy and healthy variants of anger, jealousy and envy. Therefore, it is helpful to use the modifier "unhealthy" or "dysfunctional" before anger, jealousy and envy in order to indicate that the reference is to the unhealthy version of these emotions.

According to REBT theory, the inferences at A flavour the emotion at C when rigid and extreme, or flexible and non-extreme, attitudes are held at point B. For example, a client needs to infer the presence of a threat and bring a rigid and/or extreme attitude to that inference to experience anxiety. Depression results from the inference at point A of a loss, failure or underserved plight combined with a rigid and/or extreme attitudes at B. Guilt is a function of not living up to one's moral code and/or hurting someone along with the presence of rigid

Table 2.2 Unhealthy negative emotions (UNEs) and their corresponding inferential themes in REBT theory.

Unhealthy Negative Emotions (UNEs) at C	Inferences at A: Associated major adversities
Anxiety	Threat to something important to our personal domain
Depression	Loss, failure or undeserved plight
Guilt	Breaking a moral code, failing to live up to a moral code, "hurting" someone
Shame	Falling very short of our ideal
Hurt	Someone who is important to us demonstrating that they are investing less in our relationship than we have invested or reciprocating with less than what we believe is our due
Unhealthy (dysfunctional) anger	Frustration, someone (including ourselves) transgressing our rules, someone threatening our self-esteem
Unhealthy (dysfunctional) jealousy	Someone posing a threat to an important relationship that we have
Unhealthy (dysfunctional) envy	Someone having something that we prize but do not have

attitudes and/or extreme thinking about one's behaviour. It is worth underscoring a distinguishing aspect of REBT theory: the inference at A associated with major adversities is necessary but not sufficient to produce any of the eight unhealthy negative emotions at C. The inferences in Table 2.1 above interact with rigid and extreme attitudes at point B, producing unhealthy negative emotions at point C.

Inferential themes of healthy negative emotions

You may be wondering how healthy negative emotions are conceptualized as coming into existence in the ABC model.

Like unhealthy negative emotions, the client makes the same eight inferences at point A in order to construct their healthy negative emotion at point C. However, instead of bringing to these inferences rigid and extreme attitudes, clients bring flexible and non-extreme attitudes. This combination of inferences at A and flexible and non-extreme attitudes at B result in the healthy negative emotions presented in Table 2.3.

Remember what accounts for the presence of either an unhealthy negative emotion or a healthy negative emotion at C is the presence or absence of rigid and extreme attitudes. Likewise, healthy negative emotions result from holding flexible and non-extreme attitudes towards the inferences made at A. For example, a client needs to infer a threat and bring a flexible and non-extreme attitude to that inference to experience concern. REBT, unlike other CBT models, posits that rigid

Table 2.3 Healthy negative emotions (HNEs) and their corresponding inferential themes in REBT theory.

Healthy Negative Emotions (UNEs) at C	Inferences at A: Associated major adversities
Concern	Threat to something important to our personal domain
Sadness	Loss, failure or undeserved plight
Remorse	Breaking a moral code, failing to live up to a moral code, "hurting" someone
Disappointment	Falling very short of our ideal
Sorrow	Someone who is important to us demonstrates that they are investing less in our relationship than we have invested or reciprocating with less than what we believe is our due
Healthy (functional) anger	Frustration, someone (including ourselves) transgressing our rules, someone threatening our self-esteem
Healthy (functional) jealousy	Someone posing a threat to an important relationship that we have
Healthy (functional) envy	Someone having something that we prize but do not have

attitudes are at the core of emotional disturbance and sub-sequent dysfunctional behaviour and cognitive processing. Given that REBT theory holds rigid and extreme attitudes to be at the core of emotional disturbance, it follows that psychological health and healthy negative emotions result not from inferences made at A, but from flexible and non-extreme attitudes at B. REBT therefore takes aim at rigid and extreme attitudes hoping to facilitate the development of flexible and non-extreme attitudes. It is the nature of the difference between these two sets of attitudes which we will turn our attention to in the following chapter.

3 Rigidity and flexibility in human attitudes

Foci of rigid attitudes

The three foci of rigid attitudes are one's own valued behaviour and characteristics, the valued behaviour and characteristics of other people or the valued aspects of life. All languages have ways of rigidly expressing values and preferences, and in English they are usually expressed as musts, absolute shoulds, have to's, got to's, needs and oughts. In other words, rigid attitudes are dogmatic stances about what we value.

Examples of rigid attitudes targeted for change are:

1 I must perform well in valued areas of my life.
2 I must possess certain valued characteristics like beauty and charisma.
3 You must treat me as I wish, namely fairly and with due regard of my interests.
4 The conditions of my life and those of my loved ones must include predictability, security, comfort and ample pleasures.

In these examples, the individual holding the attitude is thinking rigidly about what they value in and for themselves, in and for other people's behaviour, and in the life conditions experienced by themselves or their loved ones. These attitudes may seem to pose no risk to one's emotional well-being.

However, upon examination it becomes obvious that holding a rigid attitude will pose problems when reality does not conform to it. Inevitably fallible human beings will perform poorly in important areas of life. At one time or another, everyone has performed poorly or less than ideally. Rigidly thinking that one must perform well and then failing to do so will create the ideal conditions for emotional disturbance.

The same reasoning holds true for rigid attitudes towards others and life conditions. Note that failing to gain what we value is insufficient for emotional disturbance. REBT does not target unfulfilled values; rather, it targets rigid attitudes that suggest the values we have absolutely must be fulfilled. Take, for example, the rigid attitude that others absolutely should treat us fairly. There will inevitably come a time when other people display behaviour not meeting one's definition of fairness. When this rule of fairness is violated, it is then that the interaction between what has occurred at point A (i.e. unfairness) and one's rigid attitude at point B produces emotional disturbance at point C.

Flexible attitudes are at the core of emotional health

REBT theory argues emotional well-being and psychological health can be achieved through the development of flexible attitudes towards one's valued behaviours and characteristics, the valued behaviours of others and the valued conditions of life for us and others. As with rigid attitudes, flexible attitudes encapsulate our values. Flexible attitudes specify a preference for what is valued and explicitly negates a demand for it. This point is particularly important as newcomers to REBT often think that just the presence of a desire constitutes a flexible attitude. It does not. A flexible attitude contains a statement of what is important to us *and* an explicit negation of the rigid attitude that we must have what is important to us. This quality of flexible attitudes allows the individual holding such attitudes to accommodate problematic aspects of reality.

When this happens, healthy negative emotions at point C result from the interaction of A and B, but emotional disturbance about A is not produced. As we saw in Chapter 2, healthy negative emotions are negative in tone but are associated with constructive behaviour and realistic cognitive responses to adversity. All languages have words for expressing flexible attitudes. In English flexible attitudes are expressed, initially, with words like wish, want, desire, hope and prefer and then a negation that these must be met. Ellis & Dryden (1987) encouraged the cultivation of what they called a preferential philosophy in order to healthfully accommodate life's adversities without creating emotional disturbance.

Review these flexible attitudes:

1   I want to perform well in valued areas of my life, *but* do not have to do so.

2   I desire to possess valued characteristics like beauty and charisma, *but* do not need to possess these characteristics.

3   I would like you to treat me as I value, namely fairly and with due regard of my interests, *but*, unfortunately, you do not have to do so.

4   I hope that the conditions of my life and those of my loved ones include predictability, security, comfort and pleasures, *but* sadly these conditions do not absolutely need to exist.

Higher order preferences are more easily transformed into rigid attitudes

It is important to appreciate that our preferences are hierarchical and therefore vary in strength from mild to very strong (Dryden, 2015). Thus, we may desire support in our relationships with our friends, but more strongly value support from close family members. REBT theorizes that the stronger our preference for a particular valued behaviour, characteristic or condition, the more likely we will transform this preference into a rigid attitude. Therefore, when I mildly desire support from a friend I am less likely to transform this into a rigid attitude. Unfortunately, if my desire for support from family is very strong, I am more likely to transform this into a rigid attitude (e.g., I really want support from family and *therefore* I must get this support.) It is essential to understand that REBT theory specifies that rigidity is not qualitatively equivalent to strength of desire. Holding a very strong desire for receiving support is not equivalent to holding a rigid, absolute, dogmatic attitude for receiving it.

Rigid and extreme thinking and human biology

Another distinctive feature of REBT is the emphasis on the biological basis of irrational thinking. REBT theorizes that our tendency to hold rigid attitudes towards significant adversities seems to be more biologically based than learning based (Ellis, 1962). This is not to downplay freewill or to take an extreme deterministic position on behaviour. Nor does REBT deny the influence of culture and environment. Ellis insightfully argued that humans were born *and* reared to think irrationally. He suggested that it is largely due to our biological nature as humans that we are inclined to hold rigid attitudes towards matters that are important to us. All people easily do this about important matters and some find it much easier to do than others. Thankfully, human biology also allows for rational – that is to say flexible – attitudes. However, holding flexible attitudes tends to require cultivation through effort and practice. It is as if we are more inclined, due to our humanity, to hold rigid attitudes towards adversities and that we therefore have to go against our inherent nature in order to hold flexible attitudes when facing such adversities. Furthermore, REBT points out that nature is unfair and that some people, due to their unique biological predisposition to adopt rigid attitudes, may have to work harder, or even considerably harder, than others to hold flexible attitudes when facing adversities.

This view is not a pessimistic one. REBT is precise in how people disturb themselves and what can be done to relinquish the rigid attitudes which underpin emotional disturbance. REBT theory, however, points out that it may not be easy, and is sometimes rather difficult, for humans to maintain a flexible stance in the face of adversity, particularly with important matters.

From rigid attitudes which lie at the core of emotional disturbance come derivative or secondary attitudes which are extreme in their nature. The theory specifies three derivative extreme attitudes, namely awfulizing attitudes, discomfort intolerance attitudes and devaluation attitudes of self, others and life itself. In the next three chapters, we will turn out attention to each of these three derivative attitudes and the healthy non-extreme alternatives.

4 Awfulizing and non-awfulizing derivative attitudes

As previously explained, REBT theory holds that rigid attitudes are at the core of emotional disturbance. When we hold rigid attitudes towards adversity at point A we are likely to hold one or more of three major extreme attitudes at point B. REBT theory maintains that extreme attitudes derive from core rigid attitudes. This chapter will address a major derivative extreme attitude and its non-extreme counterpart, namely awfulizing and non-awfulizing attitudes.

Awfulizing attitudes

An awfulizing attitude is predicated on the idea that it is bad when an adversity happens to us (known as the asserted badness component). However, we take this evaluation of badness to an extreme and conclude that it is awful that the adversity has occurred (known as the asserted awfulizing component). Consider the following examples of a rigid attitude and the extreme awfulizing attitudes derived from it:

- You must treat me well. (A rigid attitude.)
- It is awful when you don't treat me well. (The extreme attitude derived from the rigid attitude.)

- I must perform well. (A rigid attitude.)
- It is terrible when I do not perform well. (The extreme attitude derived from the rigid attitude.)

- Life conditions must be as I desire them to be. (A rigid attitude.)
- It is the end of the world when life conditions are undesirable. (The extreme attitude derived from the rigid attitude.)

- I must not experience distress in response to adversity. (A rigid attitude.)
- It is awful when I experience distress in response to adversity. (The extreme attitude derived from the rigid attitude.)

In each example, the awfulizing attitude suggests:

1   No set of circumstances could be worse than the current circumstances and the inherent badness of these circumstances is without limit.
2   The set of circumstances is beyond 100% bad or wholly bad, and is on its own illogical continuum from 101% bad to infinitely bad.
3   Absolutely no good can be derived from such a limitlessly bad set of circumstances.
4   The experience cannot be transcended and one will live in this state of "awfulness" forever.

REBT theory hypothesizes that these extreme awfulizing attitudes stem from rigid attitudes which are at the core of emotional disturbance. REBT also hypotheses that non-extreme, non-awfulizing attitudes stem from the flexible attitudes a person may hold. Because flexible attitudes are at the core of emotional health, REBT encourages the adoption of flexible attitudes and non-extreme, non-awfulizing attitudes.

Non-awfulizing attitudes

A non-awfulizing attitude is a non-extreme idea about the badness of a negative event when we hold flexible attitudes towards our unfulfilled desires. Non-awfulizing attitudes have two components. These components are:

1 *An asserted badness component.* Like its awfulizing attitude counterpart, a non-awfulizing attitude is predicated on the idea that it is bad when an adversity happens to us.
2 *A negated awfulizing component.* Here it is made explicit that however bad the adversity is, it is not awful, terrible or the end of the world.

Consider the following examples of a flexible attitude and the paired non-extreme non-awfulizing attitude which stems from it:

- I want you to treat me well but you do not have to treat me well. (A flexible attitude.)
- It is bad when you don't treat me well but it is not awful. (The non-extreme derivative attitude.)

- I want to perform well but I do not have to perform well. (A flexible attitude.)
- It is bad when I do not perform well but it is not terrible. (The non-extreme derivative attitude.)

- I would like life conditions to be as I desire them to be, but unfortunately the conditions of life do not have to be as I desire them to be. (A flexible attitude.)
- It is bad when life conditions are undesirable, but it is not the end of the world when life conditions are undesirable. (The non-extreme derivative attitude.)

- I would like to not experience distress in response to adversity, but I do not have to not experience distress in response to adversity. (A flexible attitude.)

• It is bad when I experience distress in response to adversity, but it is not awful when I experience distress in response to adversity. (The non-extreme derivative attitude.)

In each example, the non-awfulizing attitude allows for or suggests:

1   Circumstances could be worse than the current circumstances, and the inherent badness of these circumstances is not without limit.
2   The set of circumstances is within the continuum of 0–100% badness.
3   Good can be derived from this bad set of circumstances.
4   The experience can be transcended.

The awfulizing attitudes discussed above, derived from core rigid attitudes, are hypothesized to play a significant role in emotional and behavioural disturbances. These extreme awfulizing attitudes are often involved in the development and maintenance of anxiety and avoidance behaviour, as well as other unhealthy negative emotions and behaviours.

Awfulizing attitudes and anxiety

In self-defeating anxiety reactions leading to avoidance behaviour, the rigid demand for flawless performance, and the derivative extreme attitude that it is awful to perform imperfectly, figure prominently. When displaying perfectionism, people often think: "Because what I am about to do is so important to me I must perform perfectly (rigid attitude) and it would be awful to perform less than perfectly (extreme awfulizing derivative attitude)." Anxiety is the subsequent emotion due to this rigid and extreme attitude, and the person is likely to avoid initiating the important task in order to avoid feeling anxious. Rumination about a poor performance and its consequences are likely. If the individual is able to initiate the performance, they will probably have highly distorted thinking about performance flaws and may suffer shame due to their rigid attitude held towards having fallen short of their ideal level of performance.

Non-awfulizing attitudes and concern

A healthier concerned response for performing well at an important task which would likely not lead to avoidance and rumination would be to hold flexible attitudes towards performing imperfectly as well as non-extreme derivative attitudes towards the possibility of performing imperfectly. A healthier response is: "Because what I am about to do is so important to me this is why I badly want to perform very well. However, I do not have to do so (flexible attitude). It would be bad to perform less than ideally (asserted badness component) but not awful (negated awfulizing component)." The latter two components comprise the non-extreme, non-awfulizing attitude.

Awfulizing and other unhealthy negative emotions

Other examples of the creation and maintenance of emotional problems can easily be found when a person applies extreme awfulizing attitudes to specific failures or rejections. For example, in the case of someone who experiences despair and depression in response to failing to gain entrance into a cherished professional educational program, they are likely to think: "Because my career is so important to me I absolutely should have been accepted into this program (rigid attitude) and therefore it is awful that I have been rejected (extreme awfulizing derivative attitude) by the admissions committee." In this case, despair and depression are experienced in response to rejection. The individual, once depressed, tends to focus on past and future failures with distorted thinking derived from their rigid and extreme attitudes towards the current rejection.

Non-awfulizing attitudes and healthy negative emotions

A healthier response to rejection would derive from flexible and non-extreme thinking about failing to get what one wants. A flexible and non-extreme mindset would go "Because my career is so important to me this is why I so strongly wanted to be accepted into this educational program but this does not mean that I absolutely should have been accepted into it (flexible attitude). It is very bad that I was not accepted into this program at this time (asserted badness component) but it is not the end of the world (negated awfulizing component)." The latter two components again comprise the non-extreme, non-awfulizing attitude. In this case, sorrow and disappointment occur in response to encountering this career rejection. The individual thinks realistically as a result of their healthy feelings of sorrow and disappointment, and focuses on what can be done going forward to learn from the experience and to increase the probability that failure will not occur in the future with subsequent applications to similar educational programs. This healthy emotional-behavioural response at point C stems from the flexible and non-extreme attitudes, at point B, which the individuals brings to the failure and rejection that has occurred to them at point A.

In the next chapter, we turn our attention to the second set of attitudes derived from rigid and flexible attitudes respectively, namely discomfort intolerance and discomfort tolerance derivative attitudes.

5 Discomfort intolerance and discomfort tolerance derivative attitudes

Discomfort intolerance attitudes

A discomfort intolerance attitude is an extreme stance towards the tolerability of an adverse event or the discomfort or distress experienced in reaction to it when our demands go unfulfilled. Consider the following examples of a rigid attitude and the extreme discomfort intolerance attitude which derives from it:

- You must treat me well. (A rigid attitude.)
- I cannot tolerate it when you don't treat me well. (A derivative extreme attitude.)

- I must perform well. (A rigid attitude.)
- I cannot bear it when I do not perform well. (A derivative extreme attitude.)

- Life conditions must be as I desire them to be. (A rigid attitude.)
- I cannot stand it when life conditions are undesirable. (A derivative extreme attitude.)

- I must not experience distress in response to adversity. (A rigid attitude.)
- I cannot withstand the distress experienced in response to adversity. (A derivative extreme attitude.)

In each example above, the discomfort intolerance attitude suggests the following:

1   That should the adverse event or the associated discomfort or distress experienced in reaction to it continue to exist, it will be impossible for me to do anything about it.
2   I will perish or succumb to either the adverse event or the associated discomfort, or to distress experienced in reaction to it.
3   I will have no ability to experience any happiness as long as the adverse event or the associated discomfort or distress experienced in reaction to it continues to exist.

REBT theory hypothesizes that flexible attitudes are at the core of emotional health. It hypothesizes that non-extreme attitudes stem from the individual's flexible attitudes. REBT encourages the adoption of flexible attitudes and non-extreme derivative attitudes.

Discomfort tolerance attitudes

A discomfort tolerance attitude is a non-extreme stance held towards the tolerability of either a frustrating event or the discomfort or distress experienced in reaction to it when our flexible attitudes go unfulfilled. Non-extreme discomfort tolerance attitudes have six components. These are:

1   An asserted struggle component
2   A negated intolerance component
3   An asserted tolerance component
4   A worth bearing component
5   A willingness to bear it component
6   A behavioural commitment to bear it component.

Consider the following examples of a flexible attitude and the paired non-extreme discomfort tolerance attitude which stems from it:

- I prefer that you treat me well but you do not have to do so. (A flexible attitude.)
- It is difficult when you do not treat me well but it is not unbearable. I can bear it, and it is worth bearing as I wish to carry on in life regardless of how well you treat me. I am willing to endure your bad treatment of me and I am going to do so. (A non-extreme derivative attitude.)

- I wish to perform well but I do not have to do so. (A flexible attitude.)

  o When I do not perform well it is very hard to tolerate, but not intolerable. I can tolerate not performing well and it is worth doing so in order to move on in life and to learn from my performance. I am willing to tolerate not performing well and I am going to do so. (A non-extreme derivative attitude.)

- I would like life conditions to be as I desire them to be, but unfortunately conditions of life do not have to be as I desire them to be. (A flexible attitude.)

  o It certainly can be very difficult to tolerate life conditions when they are not as I desire them to be, but it is not unbearable. I can stand undesirable life conditions and it is worth doing so in order to have some happiness in life despite the presence of less than ideal conditions. I am willing to endure these conditions and I am going to do so. (A non-extreme derivative attitude.)

- I would like to not experience distress in response to adversity but I do not have to not experience it. (A flexible attitude.)

  o It is difficult to withstand distress experienced in response to adversity but that does not mean that I cannot do so. I can do so and it is worth doing in order to either do something to alleviate it or to survive it until it runs its course. I am willing to tolerate this distress and I am going to do so. (A non-extreme derivative attitude.)

In each example, the discomfort tolerance attitude suggests the following:

1   That should the frustrating event or the associated discomfort or distress experienced in reaction to it continue to exist, it will not be impossible for me to do anything about it.
2   I will not perish or succumb to either the frustrating event or the associated discomfort or distressed experienced in reaction to it.
3   I have the ability to experience some happiness as long as the frustrating event or the associated discomfort or distress experienced in reaction to it continues to exist.

The discomfort intolerance attitudes discussed are known to play a significant role in emotional and behavioural disturbances. These extreme discomfort intolerance attitudes are often involved in the development and maintenance of avoidance behaviours and substance abuse disorders, as well as in virtually all emotional disorders. We will give an example of the role of discomfort intolerance attitudes in the common problem of procrastination and how to develop anti-procrastination discomfort tolerance attitudes.

Discomfort intolerance attitudes and procrastination

In self-defeating avoidance behaviours like procrastination, the rigid attitude for comfort and the derivative attitude of intolerance for discomfort usually play a prominent role. When procrastinating, people often think along the following lines: "Although I really cannot deny that it would be in my best interest to do this important work sooner rather than later, it will be uncomfortable for me to initiate effort to start it and then to maintain effort at doing it (inference at point A). I must remain comfortable (rigid attitude component) and cannot bear the discomfort of getting down to work and sustaining effort at this important work (extreme derivative attitude component of being unable to bear the discomfort of initiating and then maintaining effortful behaviour)." Discomfort anxiety is the subsequent emotion at point C and it results in procrastination, also at point C.

A healthy response to the adversity of having important work to do would be to hold flexible attitudes towards the discomfort of initiating and maintaining effort for the work as well as non-extreme derivative attitudes towards the discomfort involved in this process. A more functional set of attitudes would be along these lines: "I really cannot deny that it would be in my best interest to do this important work sooner rather than later. It will be uncomfortable for me to initiate effort to start it and then to maintain effort at doing it (inference at point A). I wish to remain comfortable while initiating this task and maintaining effort at completing it, but I do not have to remain comfortable (flexible attitude made up of an asserted preference component and a negated demand component). It will be a struggle for me to initiate effort at starting this task as well as to maintain that effort (asserted struggle component) but it is not unbearable do so (negated intolerance component). I can bear making the effort (asserted tolerance component) and it is very worthwhile for me to do so because it is important that I complete this work promptly (worth bearing component). I am also willing to bear the discomfort of making the effort of starting the task (willingness to endure component) and I commit myself to doing so (behavioural commitment to endure component). These attitudes result in feelings of healthy concern about getting this important work promptly completed. This healthy concern motivates the client to take action and then to maintain effort to complete the task.

In problems such as procrastination and other areas where intolerance of discomfort is a prominent feature, REBT mounts a concerted focus on examining both the rigid attitudes which lie at the core of emotional disturbance and the extreme discomfort intolerance attitudes which stem from these core rigid attitudes. Clients are shown how to cultivate, and to live in accord with, flexible and non-extreme attitudes. These attitudes facilitate emotional health, resiliency and tolerance for the inevitable frustrations and deprivations of life as well as the discomfort or distress experienced in reaction to these inevitable adversities. In the next chapter, attention will be turned to the final set of attitudes derived from rigid and flexible attitudes, namely devaluation attitudes and their non-extreme alternatives: acceptance attitudes.

6 Devaluation and acceptance derivative attitudes

The third and final extreme set of attitudes, termed devaluation attitudes, is hypothesized to derive from rigid attitudes at the core of emotional disturbance. Broadly speaking, the foci of these attitudes can be one's self, other people and life itself. Devaluation attitudes are extreme ideas which tend to occur when our rigid attitudes are not met. These extreme devaluation attitudes, and the rigid attitudes from which they stem, are illustrated below:

- You must treat me well. (A rigid attitude.)
- You are a bad person if you don't treat me well. (The derivative attitude.)

- I must perform well. (A rigid attitude.)
- I am less worthwhile if I do not perform well. (The derivative attitude.)

- Life conditions must be as I desire them to be. (A rigid attitude.)
- Life itself is less good when life conditions are undesirable. (The derivative attitude.)

- I must not experience distress in response to adversity. (A rigid attitude.)
- It is totally bad when I experience distress in response to adversity. (The derivative attitude.)

Rigid attitudes lead to devaluation attitudes

Devaluation attitudes derive from our rigid demands that we, others and life must be as we want them to be. They are extreme in so far as they imply:

1   A person (self or others) can be validly assigned a global rating that captures their essential value as a person. This essential worth is defined by arbitrarily chosen states that fluctuate over time. For example, a person may define their value as high when they perform very well and define their value as relatively low or absent when they perform poorly. In this case, a person's essential value fluctuates based on their performance.

2   Life can be validly assigned a total rating that validly sums up its complete nature and value. This global rating of life fluctuates up and down when certain favourable conditions of life are either present or absent.

3   That both a person and life can be validly rated or scored on the basis of a single characteristic or quality ignoring the complexity of the sum of the parts of a person or of life. This single global rating does not validly take into account the many characteristics and qualities that both a person and life itself possess.

Flexible attitudes lead to acceptance attitudes

Rational attitudes are flexible attitudes we hold towards self, others and life which, when our desires are unmet, allow for acceptance attitudes to emerge. Acceptance attitudes are non-extreme ideas which pertain to not getting what we want but don't insist that we get what we want, with regards to aspects of self, others and life itself. These acceptance attitudes stem from the flexible attitudes theorized to be at the core of psychological health. Consider the following examples where a non-extreme acceptance attitude stems from a core flexible attitude towards self, others and life conditions:

- I wish you would treat me well but you do not have to. (A flexible attitude.)
- When you do not treat me well that may be very bad but you are not a bad person. Instead, you are a fallible human who is not treating me well whom I still can accept as a person. (The non-extreme derivative attitude.)

- I really want to perform well but I do not have to perform well. (A flexible attitude.)
- When I do not perform well I am not less worthwhile as a person. Instead, my poor performance reflects the fact that I am a fallible human whom nevertheless remains acceptable as a person. (The non-extreme derivative attitude.)

- I strongly hope for life conditions that are as I desire them to be, but they sadly do not have to be as I hope they will be. (A flexible attitude.)
- Even though present life conditions are undesirable in certain ways, they are only undesirable in limited ways at this time. However, the current conditions of life do not prove that life itself is less good, and life itself nevertheless remains acceptable. Life is a complex, ever changing set of circumstances, comprised of good, neutral and sometimes bad conditions. (The non-extreme derivative attitude.)

- I wish I did not experience distress in response to adversity but such a response on my part does not have to be absent. (A flexible attitude.)
- It is bad when I experience distress in response to adversity but my total experience in life is not bad despite my current negative response. Life is a complex mix of experiences many good, others neutral and some unfortunately bad. (The non-extreme derivative attitude.)

In each example, the non-extreme acceptance attitudes possess these components:

1   An acknowledgement and a negative evaluation of a part of the self, other or life.
2   An assertion of the idea that although a part of the person or life is evaluated in a negative light, the whole cannot be similarly legitimately rated. Dryden (2015) has termed this the negation of devaluation component.
3   A declaration of the idea that when we do not get what we want this does not change the fact that people are fallible and life is complex, and that the part that is evaluated negatively does not make the whole entirely bad and therefore unacceptable.

The three components of non-extreme acceptance attitudes imply:

1   A human being cannot be validly measured or rated and assigned a single score or rating that defines their essence or worth, as far as they have it, which does not fluctuate in accord with any standard of performance.
2   Life cannot be legitimately rated with a single rating that captures its essential nature. The value of life fluctuates according to what happens at any given moment during it.
3   Both people and life have characteristics that can be legitimately rated, and such ratings may be useful endeavours of evaluation for various reasons. However, it does not make sense, nor is useful, to rate the totality of a person or of life on the basis of discrete aspects of each.

Devaluation attitudes and unhealthy negative emotions

The devaluation attitudes discussed above, deriving from rigid attitudes, are hypothesized to play a significant role in emotional and behavioural disturbances. These extreme attitudes are largely responsible for the development and maintenance of depression, guilt and dysfunctional anger amongst other unhealthy emotions. The following examples show how rigid and extreme attitudes largely produce unhealthy negative emotions like depression, guilt and anger, whereas flexible and non-extreme attitudes of acceptance allow for healthy negative feelings like sadness, remorse and healthy, functional anger.

Self-devaluation attitudes and depression

In the case of depression in response to one's poor performance, the involvement of these extreme attitudes of self-devaluation can be clearly seen. Let's assume one were to hold the following rigid attitude: "I absolutely must do well in an upcoming presentation". If, while holding this rigid attitude, the individual were to perform poorly, REBT theory would predict that feelings of depression would largely be a result of the rigid attitude demanding superb performance and the extreme, self-devaluation attitude that is derived from the rigid attitude. An example of one such extreme attitude might be "Because I did not perform well therefore I am less worthwhile as a person." However, the individual could choose to hold a flexible attitude such as "I very much wanted to perform well but I did not have to do so. I acknowledge I performed poorly but this does not mean I am less worthwhile as a person. My poor performance shows I am a fallible human but I remain acceptable as a person despite my poor performance." If the person held these flexible and non-extreme self-acceptance attitudes towards their poor performance, these would result in healthy negative feelings of sadness, sorrow, displeasure or disappointment. Note that in response to their poor performance their worth as a person would not be depreciated. They would rate their performance negatively but this negative performance rating would not lead to self-devaluation and depression.

Self-devaluation attitudes and guilt

In the case of guilt, the individual acknowledges violating some sort of moral code. The consequence of guilt stems from holding extreme attitudes derived from a rigid attitude of the self. Suppose a man held the rigid attitude "As a married man I must remain faithful to my vows of marriage" and then had an extramarital affair, REBT theory would predict that extreme attitudes of self-devaluation would produce his feelings of guilt. His devaluation attitude of the self would likely be "Because I violated my marriage vows therefore I am a bad person".[1] See if you can generate an alternative set of flexible and non-extreme, self-acceptance attitudes so that the person would experience remorse instead of guilt. We give you our version in the notes at the end of the chapter.

Other-devaluation attitudes and unhealthy anger

Another example of extreme devaluation thinking directed at another person could be seen in the case of anger. Here the individual holds a rigid attitude towards a personal transgression inflicted on them by some person. The transgressed individual would create unhealthy feelings of anger by holding a rigid attitude towards their transgressor. The rigid attitude might be "You must not commit such a transgression towards me" and REBT theory would then predict the extreme attitude of "Because you have committed such a transgression you are a rotten person, wholly bad to the core!"[2] See if you can generate an alternative set of flexible and non-extreme, other-acceptance attitudes so that the person would experience non-demanding healthy anger instead of unhealthy anger. We will give our version in the notes at the end of the chapter.

Life-devaluation attitudes and despair

Finally, extreme attitudes of life-devaluation and their emotional consequences can be seen in the individual holding a rigid attitude of how life absolutely should be. If such an individual were to hold the attitude that "my life absolutely should not have extremely difficult hardships" then that individual according to REBT theory would easily also have the attitude that "Because extreme hardship presently exists in my life this makes life itself wholly bad."[3] It would not be hard to see how such an individual would feel hopelessness and despair as a result of such rigid and extreme attitudes. Once again, see if you can develop a set of alternative flexible and non-extreme, life-acceptance attitudes so that the person would experience non-depreciating disappointment instead of despair. Again, we give our version in the notes at the end of the chapter.

In the REBT therapeutic process the first step is to identify both the core rigid attitude the individual holds as well as assess any extreme attitudes derived from it which pertain to the devaluation of self, others and life itself. Once these core and derivative attitudes are clearly identified, the therapist would then move onto interventions aimed at exposing the illogic, dysfunctional consequences and anti-empirical aspects of these attitudes. The process of how REBT therapists facilitate attitudinal change will be the focus of the remaining chapters of this newcomer's guide.

Notes

1 I really wished that I had not violated my marriage vows, but I am not immune from wrongdoing and nor do I have to have such immunity. I am not a bad person for doing so. Rather, I am an ordinary human being who acted very badly

2 The alternative set of flexible and non-extreme, other-acceptance attitudes we suggest is: "I would prefer it if you do not commit such a transgression towards me, but unfortunately you do not have to act in the way I want you to act. You are not a rotten person if you do so. Rather, you are an unrateable, fallible human being who is acting rottenly, but who is also capable of acting positively and neutrally."

3 The alternative set of flexible and non-extreme, life-acceptance attitudes we suggest is: "I would prefer it if my life does not have extremely difficult hardships, but it does not follow that it must be this way. Because extreme hardship presently exists in my life this does not make life itself wholly bad. Rather, life is highly complex comprising many positive, negative and neutral aspects".

7 REBT's distinctive therapeutic process

Psychotherapy is a psychosocial intervention. Although REBT therapists possess technical skill in rational interventions, these interventions occur within a therapeutic relationship between human beings. Although much has been written in the literature emphasizing the importance of the relationship between the therapist and her client, REBT stands alone in emphasizing both emotional empathy (accurate perception and acknowledgement of the client's feelings) and philosophical empathy (accurate perception of the inferential and attitudinal underpinnings of their problematic feelings) in this helping relationship. Philosophical empathy combined with emotional empathy leads the client to experience a deeper feeling of being accurately understood as compared to emotional empathy alone.

Like all psychotherapists, the REBT therapist communicates her capacity to perceive accurately the emotional experience of the client. However, REBT therapists avoid excessive warmth when relating to clients because clients often arrive with a dire need for love and approval, which is part of their emotional disturbance. REBT therapists try to avoid strengthening this attitude by being overly warm with the client. REBT therapists desire that clients accept themselves unconditionally and independently of the acceptance shown to them by their therapists. Secondly, by being excessively warm it is possible this warmth goes beyond laying the foundation for therapeutic trust and communicates that the client needs to be treated in a comforting fashion in order to function effectively in life. REBT therapists hope that their clients hold healthy desires for warmth and comfort from others but know that these desires will not always be met in normal human affairs. In such cases, we help clients to see that warmth and comfort from others, while desirable, are not necessary for effective functioning. That being said, the REBT therapist is not cold or at all uncaring toward the client. However, there is a fine line between being warm, caring and clinically effective on the one hand and being too warm and caring in the therapeutic relationship on the other hand, which can undermine therapeutic effectiveness.

Philosophical empathy

We mentioned philosophical empathy as being a distinctive feature of REBT. This relates to the therapist communicating her understanding of the client's attitudes, which underpin and lead to subsequent dysfunctional emotional and behavioural reactions. This understanding stems from REBT's theory of disturbance, which is that rigid and extreme attitudes are at the core of emotional disturbance. When a client discusses their emotional reactions to numerous adversities, the REBT therapist acknowledges both the healthy and unhealthy feelings clients are reporting at point C. However, in addition to this emotional empathy, the REBT therapist formulates a hypothesis, based on REBT theory, of which rigid and extreme attitudes the client is likely to be holding that underpin their unhealthy negative feelings. This hypothesis is communicated to the client to test it for accuracy. If the hypothesis does not resonate with the client, the therapist acknowledges this and, with the client's help, reformulates a new hypothesis based on REBT theory. For example, when a client reports an instance of anxiety in response to the possibility of performing poorly at some future event, the REBT therapist displays philosophical empathy by saying something like: "Might it be that your anxiety is related to holding the attitude that because there are important negative consequences associated with poor performance you must perform well?" This double-barrelled approach to empathy, namely emotional and philosophical empathy, enhances the therapeutic alliance by giving the client a rich interpersonal experience of being understood on both an emotional and a cognitive level.

Active-directive therapeutic stance

Another distinctive feature of the REBT therapeutic relationship is that the therapist adopts what is known as an active-directive therapeutic stance. This description of the stance is meant to convey that the REBT therapist actively directs the therapeutic dialogue by use of the proper balance of Socratic questions and didactic instruction. The skilled REBT therapist does not struggle with the client while taking this active-directive stance and uses all the empathic listening skills of less-directive therapists, but adds an interpersonal style that is aimed at actively and directly teaching the client the core principles and therapeutic change strategies of REBT and how to apply these to their specific emotional problem.

The REBT therapist has multiple goals in taking this flexible but active-directive stance. Foremost among these goals is teaching the client what is known in REBT as the principle of emotional responsibility. This principle is the cornerstone of REBT theory and maintains that adversity at point A may present the client with a very tempting opportunity to get upset, but it is the client's rigid and extreme attitudes towards this adversity that largely determine their unhealthy emotional and behavioural responses at point C. Through Socratic dialogue and, when necessary, didactic teaching, the therapist helps the client to appreciate the relationship between their rigid and extreme attitudes and their unhealthy emotional responses.

In order to personalize this teaching, the therapist helps the client to identify a concrete situation that they are facing which is associated with a specific unhealthy negative emotion at C. The therapist might say to a client: "In the context of the problematic situation which you have described to me, what is the most distressing aspect of this adversity associated with your reaction of despair?" This question helps the client to identify what aspect of the situation at A, the person was particularly disturbed about most (sometimes called the critical A) and confirm both the A and the C of their particular emotional problem.

Teaching the ABC model of emotion

Skilled REBT therapists know that it is important to help the client precisely identify their critical A and consequential unhealthy negative emotion C before proceeding any further. By doing this, the therapist will be best able to use Socratic dialogue to help the client identify the specific rigid and extreme basic attitudes at B which the client is likely to hold, which are largely responsible for their unhealthy emotional response at C. In REBT, the link between the client's rigid and extreme basic attitudes at point B and their consequential emotions at point C is known as the B–C connection. Clients typically enter therapy unaware or vaguely aware of the existence and importance of the B–C connection. Often, clients believe that when faced with adversity at point A, there is a direct connection to their unhealthy negative emotional response at point C. This model of emotion limits the options the client sees for effectively responding to their adversity and the associated unhealthy negative emotion. This A–C model of emotion offers only two real choices. These choices are to either eliminate the adversity at point A, which is easier said than done, or to avoid emotional experience at point C. The ways that clients typically avoid emotional experience at point C is to ingest drugs or alcohol in a short-sighted effort to numb themselves temporarily from their unhealthy negative emotion.

Alternatively, the client engages in avoidance behaviour and does not address the adversity at point A. This too has a significant downside. Not all adverse situations can, and ideally should, be avoided. Changing A would be ideal, but sadly this often cannot be done as quickly as the client would like. In the meantime, efforts to numb their emotions or failure to address adversity are likely to have significant, self-defeating, longer term consequences for the client, which are best avoided.

Prior to REBT, clients usually do not appreciate the important role that their rigid and extreme attitudes play in determining their emotional responses at point C. By teaching clients the B–C connection they come to see that they are responsible for their emotions at point C. Note that pointing out responsibility for their unhealthy negative emotions at point C is not meant to level blame at the client. The principle of emotional responsibility merely means that the client has overlooked the emotional choices which they have at point C, and which are predicated on the attitudes they are unknowingly choosing to hold at point B.

The principle of emotional responsibility

The principle of emotional responsibility liberates the client who adopts it because it offers a new option for managing their emotional responses to adversity. This option, known in REBT as the philosophical solution, means that by relinquishing their rigid and extreme basic attitudes at point B, they will then feel a healthy negative emotion at point C even when the adversity at point A continues to exist.

Once the client and the therapist agree on the precise elements of a particular ABC analysis of a specific emotional episode, the stage is then set for evaluation of the client's rigid and extreme attitudes at point B. REBT therapists are trained in three principal ways of challenging or addressing attitudes at point B. Traditionally this process has been known as disputing in REBT. This word was chosen by Ellis to convey the idea that, in a collaborative fashion, the client will be led by the therapist in an active-directive manner through a careful discussion aimed at evaluating the rigid and extreme attitudes previously agreed upon as being at the core of their emotional disturbance in the specific emotional episode being examined. Disputing does not mean an attack is directed at the client, but it does mean that the client's rigid and extreme ideas are discussed and questioned in the spirit of exposing the problems largely determined by these attitudes.

Functional, empirical and logical disputing

The principal ways of evaluating a rigid or extreme attitude are known as functional, empirical and logical disputing respectively. Each evaluative approach helps the client appreciate how their rigid and extreme attitudes are dysfunctional, anti-empirical and illogical. REBT therapists generally use more than one approach in order to thoroughly show how the client's rigid and extreme attitudes do not stand up to careful scrutiny and can be replaced with attitudes which will lead to healthy negative emotions and more functional behaviour.

Functional disputing

Functional disputing involves Socratically asking questions aiming to expose the functional emotional and behavioural consequences of two types of attitudes. Both rigid and derivative extreme attitudes are examined from the standpoint of their impact on emotional and behavioural functioning. Questions also show how alternative flexible and non-extreme attitudes would favourably impact the client's functioning. The goal is to help the client to see that there is an emotional and behavioural price is to be paid by clinging to their rigid and extreme attitudes, which would not exist if they were to relinquish these attitudes and adopt flexible and non-extreme attitudes instead. Functional disputing can be very useful in showing clients that an alternative set of attitudes will yield healthy negative emotions, which will better enable them to persist and creatively attempt to change what can be changed at point A. This can enable them to live well and enjoy some degree of happiness even when the adversity at point A cannot be changed or takes considerable time and effort to change. Functional disputing is a good way to introduce the process of disputing to the client because it shows the client the practical advantages of relinquishing their rigid and extreme attitudes, and adopting more flexible and non-extreme attitudes.

An example of functional disputing would be to evaluate the emotional and behavioural consequences of the attitude "I absolutely must perform perfectly well". The REBT therapist would pose questions aiming to show that the emotional consequences of holding this attitude are unhealthy: anxiety in advance of a performance and despair, shame or self-directed anger in the aftermath of a poor performance. The therapist would ask Socratic questions, helping the client to see the benefits of the flexible attitude "I want to perform perfectly well but I do not have to do so". The emotional consequences of holding this attitude would be healthy feelings of concern, which motivate the client to prepare in advance of the performance. These healthy feelings of concern would also optimally activate the client during the actual performance so that they have the best chance of performing well. Following a poor performance, this flexible attitude would lead the client to feel healthy feelings of disappointment, displeasure or sorrow. The relative benefits of these two sets of emotional and behavioural reactions would be examined to show the client the functional advantages of the flexible and non-extreme attitudes they could choose to adopt.

Empirical disputing

Empirical disputing aims to show the client that a careful examination of the available data will reveal that their rigid and extreme attitudes do not conform to empirical reality. For example, when a client holds the attitude "I must perform perfectly well", unbeknownst to the client no empirical data exists in support of this attitude. Socratic questioning reveals to the client that, in similar situations in the past, holding this attitude did not ensure a perfect performance. A review of this data would reveal that this attitude is inconsistent with empirical reality. The conclusion these questions would lead the client to draw is that if this attitude were empirically true, a perfect performance would always and only result. However, because this rigid attitude is not true, poor performance probably has occurred in the past and may occur again in the future. Next, the client would be led through Socratic questioning to generate an alternative flexible or non-extreme attitude which would accurately convey the empirical reality. In this case that attitude would be: "I very much want to perform perfectly well but I do not have to do so". This attitude is then examined from the standpoint of whether or not it is supported by empirical data. Therapeutic dialogue would have the client consider any instances of past poor performance. Once the client identifies past instances of poor performance, the empirical support for the new flexible attitude can be evaluated. The therapist would point out that the existence of past poor performance is empirical evidence that the attitude "I very much want to perform perfectly well but I do not have to do so" is consistent with empirical reality.

Logical disputing

The third principal way a REBT therapist might choose to help the client relinquish a rigid or extreme attitude is through Socratic dialogue aimed at exposing the inherent illogic of the attitude. For example, when a client holds the attitude that "Because I really want to perform perfectly well I absolutely must do so" a logical dispute would focus the client's attention on the logical disconnect between the premise of the attitude and the conclusion of the attitude. When we wish to perform well and do not do so it is logical to conclude that this is bad, unfortunate, inconvenient or disappointing, but it never is logical to conclude that holding a strong wish to do well necessitates that one must perform perfectly well. There is no logical connection between a desire (e.g. "I want to do perfectly well') which is not rigid and a demand (e.g. "and therefore I have to do perfectly well") which is rigid. However, a flexible conclusion (e.g. "I don't have to do perfectly well") does logically follow from the same non-rigid desire. The logical attitude "Even though I really want to perform perfectly well I do not have to do so and when I do perform poorly this is bad, unfortunate, inconvenient or disappointing" then leads to healthy negative emotions like disappointment, displeasure and sorrow, but not unhealthy negative feelings of despair, shame or self-directed anger.

Negotiating suitable homework

Once a client is shown how to replace their rigid and extreme attitudes with flexible and non-extreme attitudes, the REBT therapist will engage the client in a collaborative discussion aimed at the negotiation of a suitable homework assignment. The purpose of this assignment is to extend the work of the therapy session to the client's home environment. A well-constructed homework assignment will be somewhat challenging to the client but will not be overwhelming to carry out. Negotiating suitable homework assignments to promote therapeutic progress is an essential skill for the newcomer to develop. The aim of a well-constructed homework assignment is to help the client enhance their conviction in the flexible and non-extreme attitudes generated during the session and to implement those attitudes to modify their emotional and behavioural reactions between sessions. Homework assignments build skill at maintaining flexible and non-extreme attitudes when and where it matters most. This is essential, as there is little value if the client knows the flexible and non-extreme attitude and either does not hold it deeply or is unable to implement it outside of the session. The next two chapters discuss the importance of deepening a client's conviction in their new attitude along with the related topics of intellectual insight and emotional change.

8   Facilitating intellectual insight

The first step in psychological change involves changes in awareness. Clients entering REBT are asked to identify a specific emotional or behavioural problem which they would like to make the initial focus of treatment. Once a suitable therapeutic problem has been chosen, a specific example of it is identified in order to enable the therapist to introduce REBT's ABC model of emotion. Clients are shown that their rigid and extreme basic attitudes at point B, about the adversities they face at point A, largely lead to their self-defeating emotional and behavioural consequences at point C. Clients quickly learn what is referred to in REBT as the B–C connection, the relationship between the client's rigid and extreme attitudes and their disturbed reactions. The B–C connection applies equally to the relationship between the client's flexible and non-extreme attitudes and their subsequent healthy negative emotions and functional behaviours. This awareness is viewed as intellectual insight.

Intellectual insight is enhanced when the client begins to identify the specific rigid and extreme attitudes at point B which are used to disturb themselves about the adversity they face at point A. REBT is precise and the aim is to focus on the specific rigid and extreme attitudes that lie at the core of the client's emotional disturbance. Once these specific attitudes are identified, the client's intellectual insight is enhanced and the client and the therapist can dispute the targeted rigid and extreme attitudes as discussed earlier in this guide. Comprehensive disputing using multiple disputing methods enhances such insight.

Identifying and responding to doubts, reservations and objections

REBT therapists also facilitate client intellectual insight by soliciting and responding to clients' doubts, reservations and objections to the principles and practices of REBT. Once these doubts, reservations and objections have been effectively addressed, clients are more likely to deepen their conviction in REBT and engage in the work and practice required for change to take place. Here are some examples of clients' doubts and how to respond to them.

"I have been this way all my life"

Clients sometimes argue that because they have been a particular way all their lives, it is therefore impossible to make the changes encouraged by their REBT therapist. Clients often do not see the non-sequitur in their thinking. In response, the REBT therapist may consider the hypothesis that the client's discomfort intolerance attitude is behind this objection. Therefore, the therapist will point out that entrenched ways of thinking and feeling, and behaviour, necessitate greater effort, time and practice to change in comparison to less entrenched patterns. It is never logical to conclude that the length of time a cognitive-emotive-behavioural pattern has existed makes it impossible to modify. The REBT therapist can raise the hypothesis that what the client holds is the basic attitude that it is too hard for them to do the required work. REBT therapists then do a cost-benefit analysis with the client and help the client to see that although the cost of change is great, the benefit makes the sustained effort worth pursuing.

"Rational attitudes only apply to insignificant adversities, not significant ones"

Clients may argue that REBT can only be applied to relatively insignificant matters in life and that flexible and non-extreme thinking cannot be applied to very important adversities. To effectively address this objection, the REBT therapist first has to engage in some therapeutic work of her own. It is quite hard to teach a client that one can achieve philosophical acceptance of a great loss, for example, when the therapist believes the loss absolutely should not occur and is horrible or unbearable. Once the therapist has thought through and worked on replacing her own rigid and extreme attitudes towards the very difficult adversity her client is facing, she can more convincingly dispute the client's attitudes towards that very same issue. If the therapist has faced a similar adversity in the past, the therapist can discuss the client's objection by disclosing how she eventually came to accept the difficult adversity now facing the client. Ellis emphasized that the best REBT therapists were those who genuinely practised REBT on themselves. By learning to accept the "bitter pills" of life and see difficult losses as painful but bearable, the therapist can authentically model philosophical acceptance based on flexible and non-extreme thinking. With empathy and authenticity, the therapist can discuss a very bad event as truly bad but not awful. In discussing a client's doubts on this matter, the therapist answers the objection in an open, honest and logical way, without demanding that the client immediately agree while encouraging the client to relinquish their doubt in the application of REBT to the most significant matters of life.

Construing irrational attitudes positively and rational attitudes negatively

When clients first encounter irrational attitudes and rational attitudes, they often think that some irrational attitudes are in fact positive and some rational attitudes are negative. A common misconception, for example, is that a person needs to hold a demanding attitude towards success, otherwise they will not be motivated to do anything. The REBT therapist explains that what motivates the person is their desire for success and that that this desire can be kept flexible or made rigid. When it is made rigid, the person is still motivated by their desire but the rigid component drags them back since it is that component that is at the core of disturbance. When the person keeps their desire flexible, the desire is again motivating and the flexibility means that the desire can be acted on without disturbance. Another misconception is that "acceptance" means resignation. Actually, the rational concept of acceptance acknowledges the reality of the existing state of affairs and that, if possible, the factors involved can be changed so that the situation itself can be changed, which is the antithesis of resignation.

The difference between intellectual insight and emotional change

Once clients' doubts have been dealt with, REBT therapists teach them to understand the difference between intellectual insight and emotional change. Emotional change was initially discussed by Ellis (1963) and, along with behavioural change, is one of the true goals of REBT. This distinction is yet another step in enhancing intellectual insight. The goal of this discussion is to have the client appreciate the necessity of going beyond mere intellectual insight, to change their unhealthy negative emotions to healthy negative emotions and to change dysfunctional behaviour to functional behaviour. Intellectual insight which is not followed by emotional change is essentially useless. Intellectual insight is far easier to achieve than emotional change largely because little discomfort is encountered in achieving it. Intellectual insight is enhanced by reading books on REBT or listening to audio and video presentations like those (found at REBTDoctor.com) on the theory and practice of REBT while emotional change cannot be achieved in this passive way. Emotional change usually involves some degree of discomfort to be achieved and will be the focus of our attention in the next chapter.

9   Emotional change follows intellectual insight

In REBT, emphasis is placed on the development of emotional change. Emotional change was defined by Ellis (1963) as the client coming to possess a deep conviction in the functional utility, empirical validity and logical nature of the flexible and non-extreme attitudes which are required for improved emotional and behavioural functioning. The client who has made an emotional change has also developed a deep conviction that his irrational attitudes produce dysfunctional behaviours, are inconsistent with reality and illogical in nature. This deep conviction leads to a change in emotions from unhealthy negative emotions to healthy negative emotions. Having achieved emotional change, the client has come to learn to feel healthy negative emotions (C) in response to particular adversities (A) and is capable of acting in ways that are consistent with the newly adopted flexible and non-extreme attitudes.

Consider a client who claims to have made an emotional change with regard to his unhealthy feelings of depression in response to being out of work. Prior to his emotional change, the client's unhealthy feelings of depression block him from consistently submitting applications for employment. Once an emotional change has occurred, the client begins to submit applications for employment on a consistent basis. He feels the healthy negative emotions of sadness and disappointment each time he submits an application and does not subsequently receive an invitation to interview for the position. The emotional change he has achieved is a consequence of a rational attitude like "I really want to find a good job quickly and easily but I do not have to do so." The evidence for the presence of this flexible rational attitude is that his healthy feelings of sadness and disappointment in response to each rejection do not lead to the cessation of his attempts to continue to search for a job. His persistence in the face of continued rejection reflects the emotional change achieved.

Now consider a client who suffers from unhealthy anxiety at the prospect of being rejected by a woman. Prior to the development of an emotional change, the client might give lip service to the rational idea that it is bad but not awful to be rejected. With this extreme attitude, the client would feel the unhealthy negative emotion of anxiety. He would continue to avoid requesting a date. However, once the client has achieved an emotional change he would feel the healthy negative emotion of concern that he might be rejected but would demonstrate the existence of an emotional change by risking rejection by asking someone out on a date.

Homework leads to emotional change

These examples show evidence that an emotional change has taken place is that the client is able to execute behavioural changes in the real world which reflect the adoption of rational attitudes and the existence of healthy negative emotions. These behavioural changes are developed through the execution of agreed upon homework assignments.

There are essentially four types of homework assignments, namely cognitive, imaginal, emotive and behavioural assignments. All will help the client change unhealthy negative feelings, rigid and extreme attitudes, unhealthy negative feelings and self-defeating behaviours because attitudes, feelings and behaviours are interactive phenomena within the individual. Cognitive, imaginal and emotive homework assignments largely set the stage for executing behavioural homework assignments, which are an important path to emotional and behavioural change. Cognitive assignments include activities like completing a REBT self-help form by identifying irrational attitudes, coming up with arguments to expose the dysfunctional consequences, the anti-empirical and illogical characteristics of these attitudes and then constructing rational alternative attitudes to adopt. Imaginal homework assignments are when the client imagines acting while holding a flexible and non-extreme attitude. Emotive homework assignments include activities like Rational-Emotive Imagery which require that the client imagine a dreaded activating event: after initially emoting in their usual dysfunctional way, the client transforms his usual unhealthy negative emotion into a healthy negative emotional response while holding in mind the adversity (A). This assignment provides a corrective emotional experience, albeit an imagined one. Behavioural homework assignments, usually the best type of assignments for efficiently facilitating emotional change, are activities where the client actually acts in ways that are consistent with his rational attitudes and sees first-hand that the rational attitudes produce improved functioning in the real world. Having analysed the irrational nature of their attitudes by completing self-help forms and having rehearsed rational thinking and experienced healthy negative emotions through the practice of Rational-Emotive Imagery, the client is better prepared to do what is most difficult which is to act in a way that is consistent with the alternative rational attitude that has been rehearsed. It is only through action that enduring emotional change occurs.

Emotional change is considerably harder to obtain than intellectual insight. Its development requires considerable effort, tolerance of discomfort and the willingness to engage in unfamiliar ways of thinking, feeling and behaving. Emotional change requires work and practice, and it is best achieved by using a combination of cognitive, imaginal, emotive and behavioural strategies.

Discomfort disturbance blocks emotional change

Clients often have difficulty making emotional changes. When this occurs, the client and therapist examine the reasons for this occurrence. More often than not, clients hold rigid and extreme attitudes, leading to what in REBT is called discomfort disturbance. Here the client believes that the discomfort involved in doing the agreed upon homework, which will usher in emotional change is too hard, too unfamiliar or in some other way unbearable. REBT therapists then target these self-defeating attitudes for change to facilitate the implementation of homework, which, in time, will weaken the client's conviction in their irrational attitudes and deepen their conviction in rational attitudes, leading to emotional change.

The development of emotional change requires the willingness to leave one's comfort zone, go against the grain of one's typical ways of reacting and try new ways of responding cognitively, emotively and behaviourally. Once a client experiences emotional change, the behaviours and attitudes that produced it have to be practised in order for emotional change to be maintained. REBT theory holds that fallible humans are predisposed to returning to self-defeating rigid and extreme attitudes, unhealthy negative emotions and the associated self-defeating behaviours. It is only when a client demonstrates a willingness to exert continued effort to maintain the hard fought gains of therapy that one can be confident of the firm establishment of emotional change. In the final chapter of this guide, we will conclude with a discussion of how a client maintains and preferably extends his treatment gains after the formal course of therapy sessions has come to an end.

10 Teaching clients to become their own REBT therapist

The principle of emotional responsibility provides the foundation for our work with clients. We want to show clients how they can largely determine their emotional destiny through self-directed efforts to adopt and then maintain healthy, flexible, non-extreme attitudes. Albert Ellis was an exceptionally self-directed individual and the theory of REBT places a strong emphasis on personal responsibility, self-acceptance and self-direction. REBT strives to teach clients to become personally responsible for their emotional and behavioural reactions in response to the adversities of life. We teach clients to accept themselves unconditionally even when others reject them or disapprove of them. We encourage people to be self-directed in pursuing their idiosyncratic, vitally absorbing interests that will give their lives meaning and maximize their personal happiness over the course of their lifetime.

REBT therapists encourage self-therapy

It would be hypocritical for the REBT therapist to teach these ideas on the one hand while fostering dependency on the therapeutic process on the other hand. Therefore, from the outset of therapy, REBT therapists are striving to convey to clients that at the end of formal therapy sessions it is hoped that a few things will occur. First, it is strongly desired that once clients make treatment gains they will maintain them. Second, we hope that clients learn to extend their treatment gains to new areas in a continued effort to self-actualize. Third, we encourage clients to assume responsibility for becoming their own REBT therapists.

Preparing clients to respond to lapses

REBT therapists prepare clients for lapses and relapses before therapy has ended. We encourage clients to see themselves as fallible human beings and not to disturb themselves by rating themselves should they have a lapse (which we define as a partial return to a problem state). Clients are encouraged to rate their lapse as self-defeating but to continue to accept themselves unconditionally despite its occurrence. This helps the client not to deny the existence of the lapse and to address the attitudes that gave rise to it before it becomes a full blown relapse. Hopelessness is averted by teaching the client to avoid demanding perfection but not to go to the other extreme of resigning themselves to indulgent, self-defeating behaviour. It is hoped that a client has made a profound philosophical change as a result of REBT, and that when a lapse or backsliding occurs the client will merely acknowledge it. Then, having acknowledged their backsliding, the client will immediately do what it takes to restore their treatment gains using the relevant principles and practices taught to them when they were actively participating in therapy.

Independent continued use of the ABC model

REBT therapists want their clients to evolve into their own therapists, in effect to think like an REBT therapist and to continually use the ABC framework to analyse their disturbed emotional and behavioural reactions. We want clients to continue to identify their rigid and extreme attitudes and to question these attitudes on their own, and then to devise empowering flexible and non-extreme attitudes just as their therapists helped them to do during the formal phase of therapy. We want clients to maintain the philosophical change that occurred during the course of therapy and to strengthen it through self-directed therapeutic activities. Some of these activities can be the continued use of REBT self-report forms, Rational-Emotive Imagery and self-assigned behavioural homework assignments. Another good way of strengthening and extending treatment gains is to strive to be a good model of REBT philosophy to friends and family. This translates into concrete behaviours like refraining from rating people when others misbehave and modelling tolerance for themselves, others and life. When the client becomes a model of the philosophy on which REBT is built, they are not merely talking the rational talk but walking the rational walk for themselves and for others. This might mean showing others how to accept themselves, warts and all, and then to strive to change those things about themselves that can be changed. Teaching others the philosophy of REBT is a good way to keep it fresh in one's mind and to see how it can be applied to new problems not necessarily covered during the course of therapy. This does not mean that clients are urged to "convert" friends or family or to go on a rational crusade. What it means is showing others the emotional options they have when adversities occur. It can mean talking about REBT in a formal way to friends or family, or it can mean something as simple as talking about the value of tolerance for one's self or others in an informal way.

Psychological fitness is like physical fitness

We would like to close this Newcomer's Guide with a metaphor. Flexibility, discomfort tolerance and unconditional acceptance of self and others are very much like physical fitness. The human condition is such that we need to actively do things to maintain our rational fitness just as we need to do things to maintain physical fitness. Fallible humans may have a preference for effort-free rationality but they would be well advised not to demand it! Which is just as well, as effortless approaches to becoming rational and therefore more psychologically healthy, sadly, do not exist, in all probability. On the other hand, if clients are prepared to make effortful use of REBT then they may well surprise themselves at what they can achieve!

References

Beck, A.T. (1976) *Cognitive therapy and the emotional disorders.* New York: International Universities Press.

Dryden, W. (2009) *Understanding emotional problems: The REBT Perspective.* Hove, East Sussex: Routledge.

Dryden, W. (2015) *Rational emotive behaviour therapy: Distinctive features. 2nd edition.* Hove, East Sussex: Routledge.

Ellis, A. (1962) *Reason and emotion in psychotherapy.* New York: Lyle Stuart.

Ellis, A. (1963) Toward a more precise definition of 'emotional' and 'intellectual' insight. *Psychological Reports, 13,* 125–126.

Ellis A., & Dryden, W. (1987) *The practice of rational-emotive therapy.* New York: Springer.

Index

ABC model 5–8, 44–5
acceptance attitudes 34–6, 53
active-directive therapeutic stance
43–4, 46
adversity: avoidance behaviours
5–6, 24, 30, 45; awfulizing
attitudes 21–2; changing
7–8; devaluation attitudes 34;
discomfort intolerance attitudes
27; inferential themes 12;
insignificant versus significant
adversities 53; and the principle
of emotional responsibility 43–4
American Psychological
Association 1
anger: and extreme behaviour 9;
healthy (functional) anger 11,
13; other-devaluation attitudes
38; unhealthy (dysfunctional)
anger 11, 12
anti-procrastination attitudes 30–2
anxiety: and awfulizing attitudes
24–5; and emotional change
58; inferential themes of 12;
as unhealthy negative emotion
(UNE) 11
approval, desire for 41
asserted awfulizing components
21–2
asserted badness components 21–2,
23, 25, 26
asserted preference components 31
asserted struggle components 28, 31

asserted tolerance components 28, 31
avoidance behaviours 5–6, 24, 30, 45
awfulizing attitudes 21–2, 24–5

basic attitudes: and future events 7–8;
initially addressing 6; and past
events 7; of therapists 8; see also
flexible and non-extreme attitudes;
rigid and extreme attitudes
B-C connection 44, 45, 51
Beck, Aaron T. 1, 5
behavioural change, as goal of
REBT 54
behavioural commitment to bear it
components 28, 31
behavioural homework 59
biased inferences 5
biology, and rigid attitudes 18–19

cognitive distortions 5, 10
cognitive homework 58–9
concern: as healthy negative
emotion (HNE) 11, 47;
inferential themes 13; and non-
awfulizing attitudes 25
constructive behaviour 17
cost-benefit analyses 52–3
creative problem solving, lack of 9

devaluation attitudes 33–4, 36–9
depression: and awfulizing attitudes
25; and devaluation attitudes
37; and emotional change 57–8;

Printed in the United States
by Baker & Taylor Publisher Services